When A Best Friend is Lost
By
Dr. Monica Diedrich with Colleen Fox
illustrations by www.BMcreativestudios.com
www.petcommunicator.com

THIS BOOK IS DEDICATED TO ALL CHILDREN AND IN PARTICULAR MY YOUNGER GRANDCHILDREN

Emma, Bella, Haley and Zac

Dr. Monica is an Animal Communicator who listens to, and communicates with pets all over the world.

This is a true story of a dog who goes out of a friend's yard to look for his parents and is lost far away from home. It is also a story about never giving up the search for your lost pet and the kindness of strangers.
It is a story of being lost but finding his way back home too. A story of hope and perseverance.

THE NAME OF THIS DOG
WAS SIMPLY "SPIKE"
AND HE LIVED IN A HOUSE
WITH PLENTY OF HYPE.

A MOM AND A DAD,
TWO GIRLS AND TWO BOYS,
A DOG AND THREE KITTENS,
A HOUSE FULL OF JOY.

2

BUT THAT WASN'T ALL
OF THE FAMILY, YOU SEE.
THERE WERE REPTILES AND TURTLES,
AND BIRDS IN TALL TREES.

3

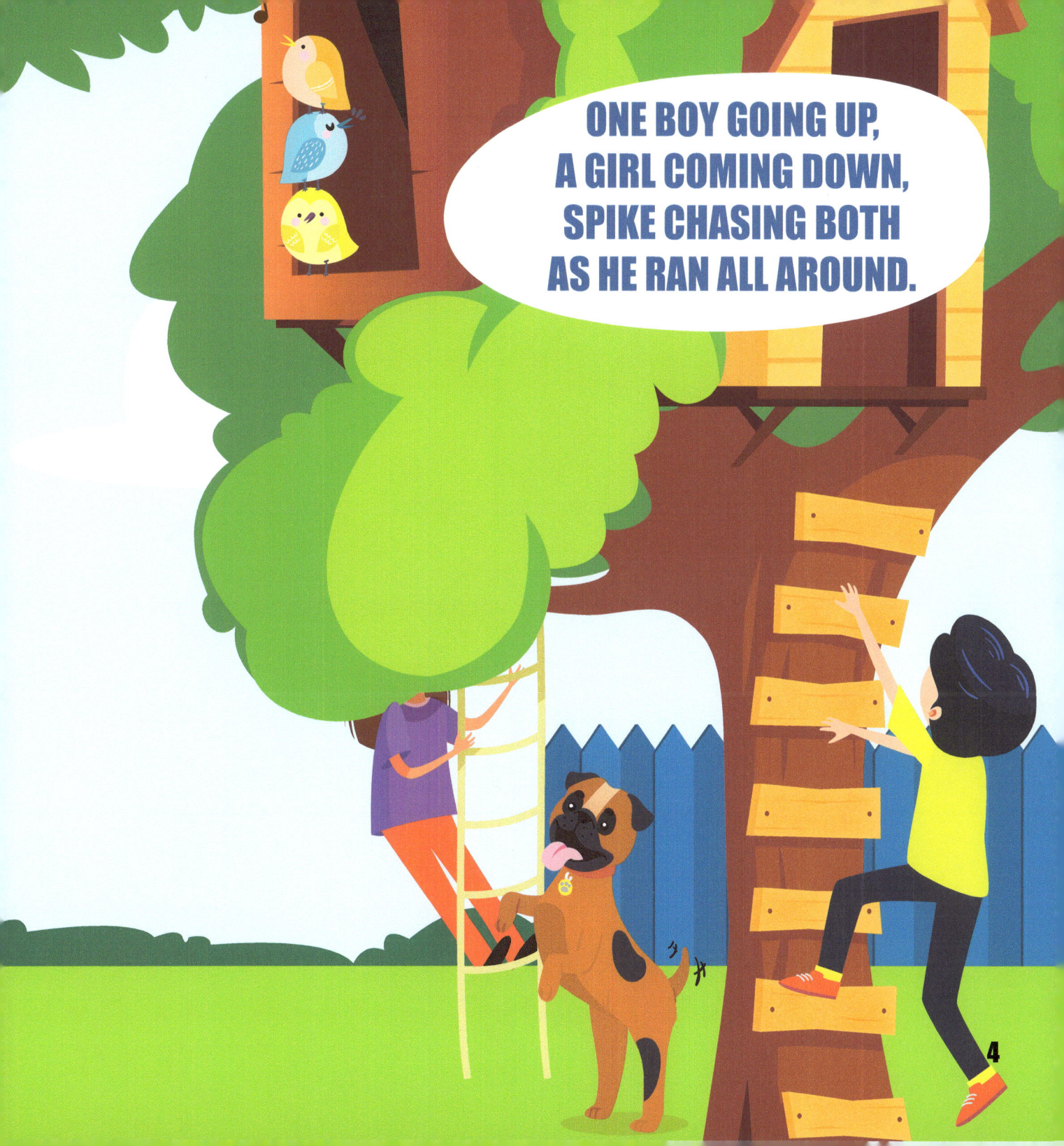

ONE BOY GOING UP,
A GIRL COMING DOWN,
SPIKE CHASING BOTH
AS HE RAN ALL AROUND.

4

BIRDS SCREECHING AND CHIRPING,
CATS CLIMBING THE WALL,
EVERYONE BUSY
BUT HAVING A BALL!

6

SPIKE LOVED TO GO DRIVING
TO GET COFFEE WITH DAD,
SAME TIME EVERY MORNING
ALWAYS HAPPY, NEVER SAD.

THE CAR WINDOW WAS DOWN,
HIS NOSE IN THE AIR,
HIS TAIL WAGGING WILDLY
WITH NEVER A CARE.

SPIKE WAS A BOXER
WITH PLENTY TO SAY.
I KNOW 'CUZ WE TALKED
FOR HOURS ONE DAY.

I'M LONELY

9

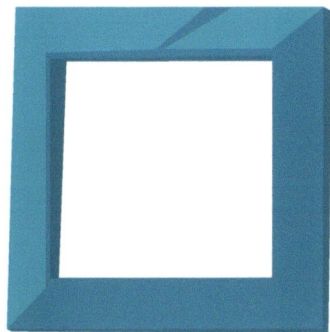

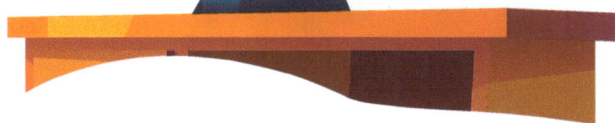

HE TOLD ME HE WAS LONELY
WHEN DAD WENT AWAY,
AND WANTED SOME COMPANY
TO CUDDLE AND PLAY.

10

SO A NEW FRIEND FOR SPIKE
MOM LOOKED FOR ONE DAY.
SHE SOON BROUGHT HER HOME
SO THE TWO DOGS COULD PLAY.

11

THEY GAVE HER A NAME
AS SWEET AS SHE WAS,
A RARE AND PERFECT "JASMINE"
LIKE THE FLOWERS MOM LOVES.

JASMINE AND SPIKE
THEY HAD SO MUCH FUN
DOING THINGS TOGETHER
WITH PLACES TO RUN.

13

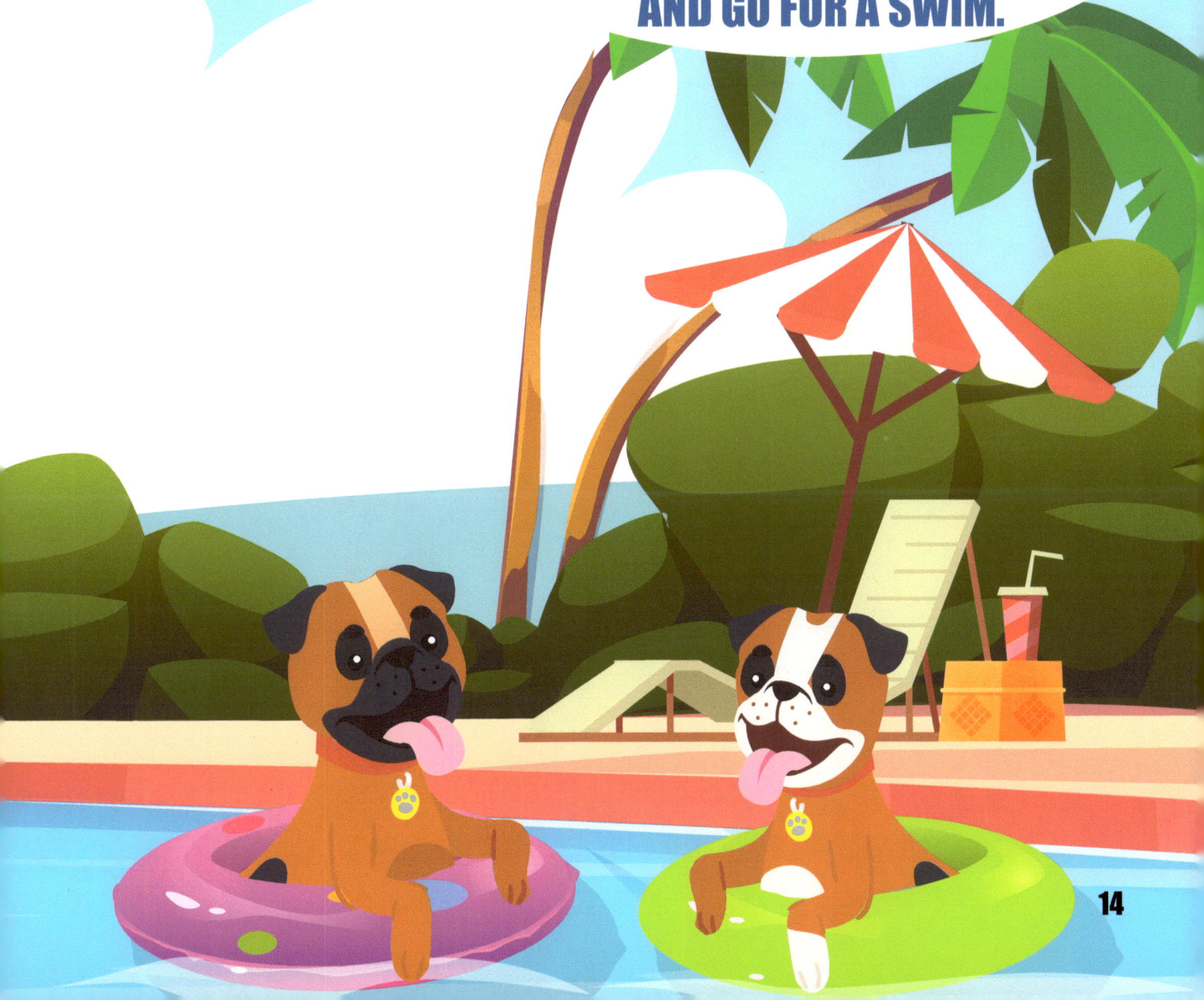

THEN ONE SUNNY DAY
SPIKE WENT ON AN OUTING
WITH DAD'S GROWN-UP SON
WHO LOVED TO GO HUNTING.

DOWN FROM THE MOUNTAIN
THE HUNT CAME TO AN END.
THE SON STOPPED TO REST
AT THE HOUSE OF A FRIEND.

16

THEY TALKED AND THEY LAUGHED
AND THEY HAD SO MUCH FUN.
THEY SLEPT THROUGH THE NIGHT
'TIL AWAKENED BY THE SUN.

MEANWHILE POOR SPIKE
WAS ALONE THROUGH THE NIGHT,
OUTSIDE IN THE YARD
WITH NO ONE IN SIGHT.

18

HE WAS TIRED AND COLD,
HE WANTED SOME FOOD,
AND SOME PEOPLE TO PET HIM
TO MAKE HIM FEEL GOOD.

20

BY EARLY IN THE MORNING
HE'D HAD QUITE ENOUGH.
HE CLIMBED OVER THE FENCE AND
LEFT WITH A HUFF.

22

SPIKE'S MOM THEN CALLED ME. SHE WAS FRUSTRATED AND SAD. "MY SON HAS LOST SPIKE, AND I'M GOING MAD!

23

"PLEASE HELP US," SHE SAID, "I KNOW YOU CAN SEE THE PICTURES HE SENDS OF WHERE HE COULD BE."

24

"WE LOVE HIM SO MUCH, OH, PLEASE TELL HIM SO. WE MISS HIM MUCH MORE THAN HE'LL EVER KNOW."

25

"IT'S HARD NOT TO CRY
WHEN WE KNOW THAT HE'S LOST,
BUT IF YOU HELP HIM COME BACK
THEN OUR TEARS WILL TURN OFF."

26

i love my family

I TALK WITH DEAR PETS
OF MANY DIFFERENT KINDS.
IT'S VERY SPECIAL WORK,
THE VERY BEST I COULD FIND.

27

SINCE THE TIME I WAS LITTLE
I REALIZED THEN
I COULD TALK TO DOGS
AND TO KITTENS AND HENS.

28

WHEN I WAS STILL LITTLE,
TELLING GROWNUPS WAS SCARY.
IF I COULD TALK TO ANIMALS
IT MADE THEM VERY WARY.

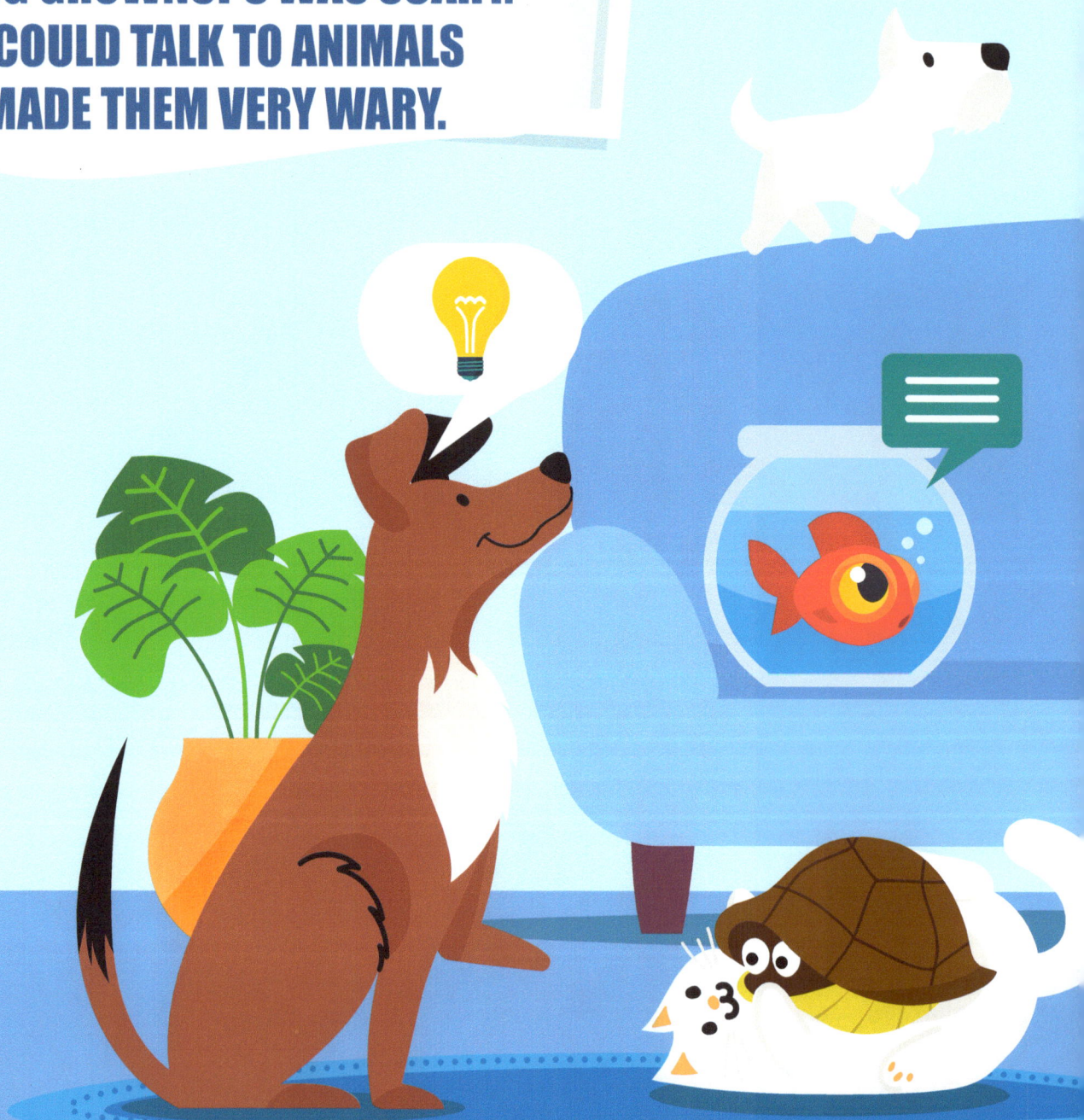

29

BUT NOW I'M A GRANDMA
AND I CAN SAY IT OUT LOUD.
I TALK TO THE ANIMALS
EVERY DAY AND I'M PROUD!

30

BUT HOW DO I HELP
A LOST DOG LIKE SPIKE?
I USE PICTURES AND THOUGHTS
THAT DOGS SEE AND LIKE.

31

I'M LOST
THEY TALK BACK WITH PICTURES
I SEE IN MY HEAD.
JUST LIKE CARTOONS,
I CAN READ WHAT THEY SAID.

WHEN I TALK WITH ANIMALS,
THEY TELL ME THEIR NEEDS,
THEIR FEELINGS, THEIR SECRETS,
THEIR WISHES, THEIR DEEDS.

THE PICTURES HE SENT ME
SHOWED THE PLACES HE'D BEEN,
THE FEELINGS HE FELT,
AND THE SPOT HE WAS IN.

36

IN A PICTURE SPIKE SENT ME HE WAS CLOSE TO THE FENCE BY A NICE LADY'S HOUSE, BUT NOTHING MADE SENSE.

WHEN I TOLD THIS TO HIS MOM,
ON STREETS ALL AROUND
SHE PUT UP BIG SIGNS
HOPING HE'D QUICKLY BE FOUND.

39

SHE ALERTED THE SHELTERS
AND TOLD RESCUE GROUPS, TOO.
NEIGHBORS AND FRIENDS
KNEW SPIKE WAS LONG OVERDUE.

40

SHE'D TOLD EVERYONE
BY THE END OF THE WEEK,
BUT SHE WORRIED AND WONDERED.
THE OUTLOOK WAS BLEAK!

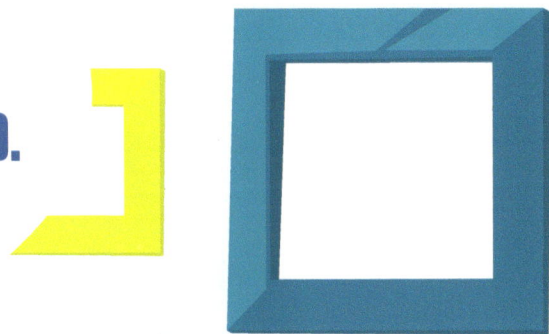

IT STARTED TO RAIN
AND THE TEMPERATURES DROPPED.
NO ONE HAD SEEN HIM
SINCE THE DAY HE WALKED OFF.

I TALKED TO SPIKE
WITH PICTURES IN MY MIND,
WISHING AND HOPING
THAT HE WAS STILL FINE.

I TOLD HIM, "DON'T FEAR.
JUST MAKE YOURSELF SEEN
BY THE VERY KIND LADY
WHOSE HOUSE YOU ARE NEAR."

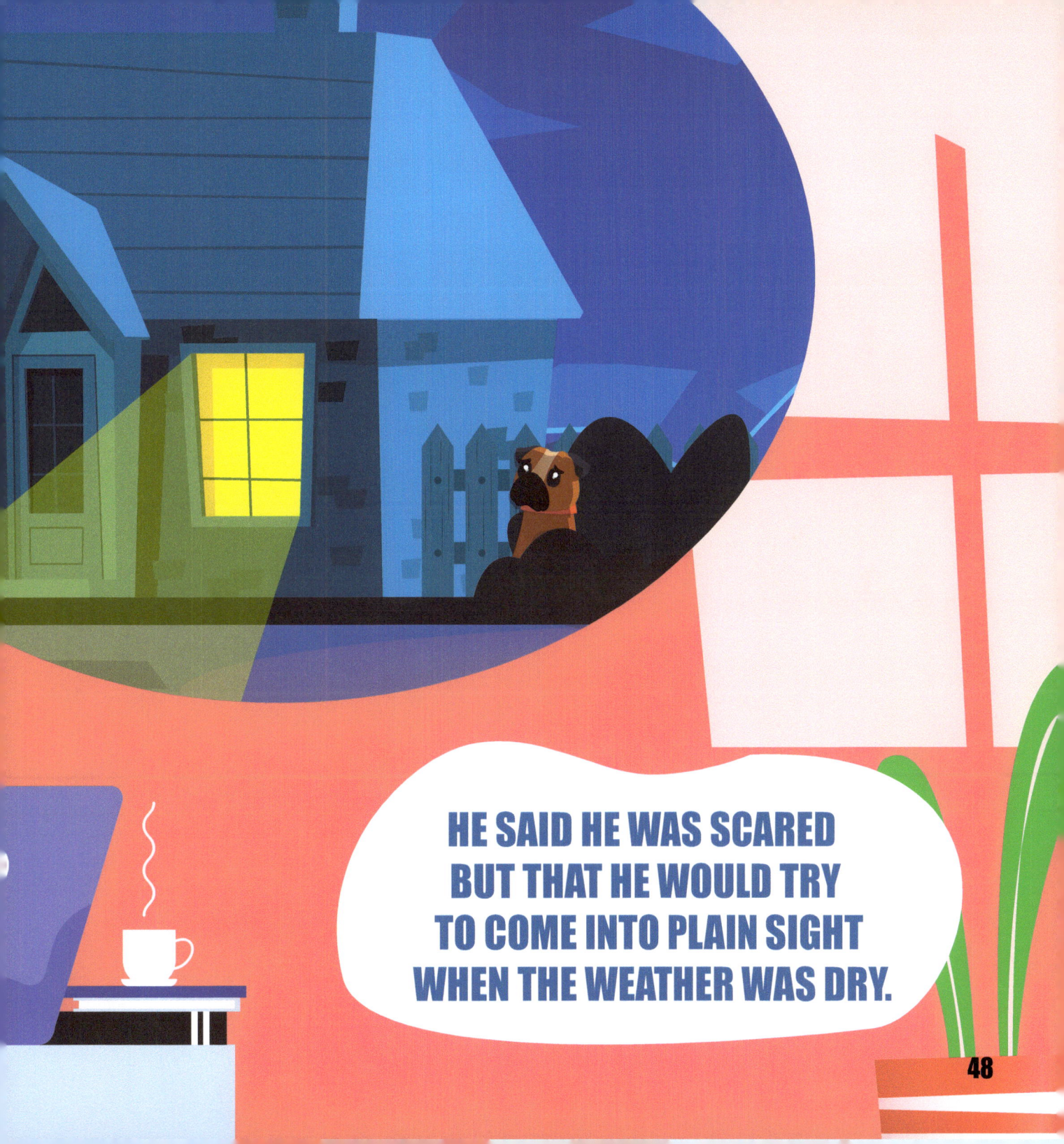

HE SAID HE WAS SCARED
BUT THAT HE WOULD TRY
TO COME INTO PLAIN SIGHT
WHEN THE WEATHER WAS DRY.

THEN THE NICE LADY SAW
FROM THE CORNER OF HER EYE
THAT A TIRED AND HUNGRY DOG
WAS HIDING NEARBY.

SHE CALLED RIGHT AWAY
THE NUMBER SHE FOUND
ON THE POSTERS THEY'D PUT
ON EVERY LIGHT POST IN TOWN.

MISSI

FROM A FAR AWAY PLACE SPIKE'S MOM CAME IN TO THE NICE LADY'S HOUSE TO GO SEARCHING FOR HIM.

SHE CALLED, "SPIKE WHERE ARE YOU?"
I'VE COME HERE TO SEE
IF THE DOG THE LADY SPOTTED
IS MY OWN RUNNING FREE.

SHE CALLED LOUDER AND LOUDER
AS THE CAR INCHED ON BY
UNTIL AT LAST SHE STOPPED
'CUZ SHE THOUGHT SHE HEARD A CRY.

53

"SPIKE, IS THAT YOU?" SHE SAID, "MAKING THOSE SOUNDS?" SHE SHED TEARS OF JOY BECAUSE HER DOG HAD BEEN FOUND.

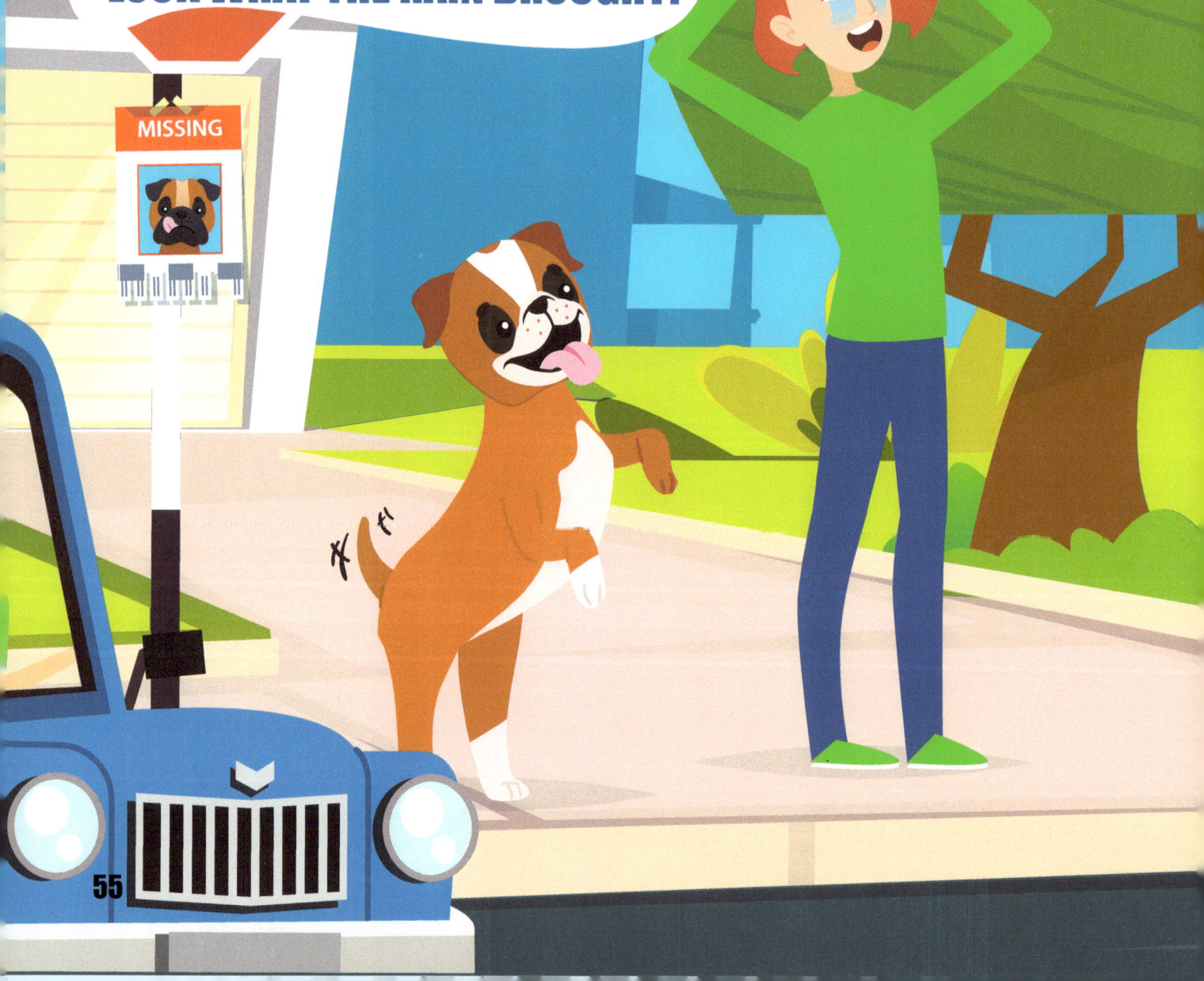

HE CAME RUNNING SO FAST AS SOON AS HE COULD SEE HIS MOM AND HIS JASMINE STOPPED NEAR A TREE.

MOM HUGGED HIM AND KISSED HIM
AND JASMINE DID TOO.
SPIKE WAS NOW BACK
WITH THE BEST FRIENDS HE KNEW.

MISSING

57

THEY THANKED THE NICE LADY WHO MADE THE PHONE CALL, THEN THEY JUMPED IN THE CAR WHERE HE FOUND HIS OLD BALL.

58

WHILE DRIVING STRAIGHT HOME
THEY WENT PAST THE STREET
WHERE THEY ALWAYS WOULD GET HIM
HIS MOST FAVORITE TREAT.

59

MOM STOPPED TO BUY HIM
HIS FAVORITE CUISINE.
TEN HAMBURGERS SHE GAVE HIM.
MORE THAN HE'D EVER SEEN!

AT HOME SAFE AND SOUND,
THEIR PROMISES WERE SENT
NEVER TO LEAVE SPIKE ALONE
WHEREVER THEY WENT.

62

Dr. Monica is an Animal Communicator who listens to, and communicates with pets all over the world.

This is a true story of a dog who goes out of a friend's yard to look for his parents and is lost far away from home. It is also a story about never giving up the search for your lost pet and the kindness of strangers.
It is a story of being lost but finding his way back home too. A story of hope and perseverance.

www.ingramcontent.com/pod-product-compliance
Lightning Source LLC
Chambersburg PA
CBHW061048090426
42740CB00002B/76